GEORGE WASHINGTON CARVER

Nature's Trailblazer

GEORGE WASHINGTON CARVER

Nature's Trailblazer

Teresa Rogers

Interior Illustrations by Antonio Castro
Cover Art by Larry Raymond

Twenty-First Century Books

A Division of Henry Holt and Co., Inc.

Frederick, Maryland

Published by
Twenty-First Century Books
A Division of Henry Holt and Co., Inc.
38 South Market Street
Frederick, Maryland 21701

Printed in Mexico

10 9 8 7 6 5 4 3 2 1

Library of Congress Cataloging in Publication Data

Rogers, Teresa
George Washington Carver: Nature's Trailblazer

(An Earth Keepers Book)
Includes glossary and index.
Summary: Examines the life and accomplishments of the black scientist
famed for his agricultural research and innovations.
1. Carver, George Washington, 1864?-1943—Juvenile literature.
2. Afro-American agriculturists—Biography—Juvenile literature.
3. Agriculturists—United States—Biography—Juvenile literature.
4. Afro-Americans—Biography—Juvenile literature. [1. Carver, George
Washington, 1864?-1943. 2. Agriculturists. 3. Afro-Americans—Biography.]
I. Castro, Antonio, ill. II. Title.
III. Series: Earth Keepers
S417.C3R58   1992
630'.92—dc20 [B] 91-45259 CIP AC
ISBN 0-8050-2115-9

CONTENTS

"I am not a finisher. I am a blazer of trails."

Chapter 1

A Blazer of Trails

On October 8, 1896, a train pulled out of the station at Ames, Iowa. It headed south through fertile farmland. From one of the windows in the train's third-class car, a tall, thin black man watched the passing scenes. Autumn trees made splashes of bright color against the acres of warm, golden cornstalks.

Whenever the train stopped at stations along the way, the passenger took notice of the farmers bringing their wagonloads of harvested crops to market. The passenger's name was George Washington Carver, and he had begun the 1,000-mile journey to Tuskegee, Alabama.

Carver had recently accepted a teaching position there at the Tuskegee Institute. He had been hired to teach new farming methods at the Institute's agriculture school.

As the train traveled through the countryside of the South, George Carver could see that such instruction was badly needed. Outside his window, he reported, there was nothing but "barren and furrowed hillsides and wasted valleys." The land was riddled with deep gullies.

Carver knew at once that wasteful farming techniques had caused the problem. For most of his life, he had been learning and teaching others about nature. As a boy, he spent many days exploring the forests and prairies around his home. As an agriculture student and researcher, he came to see that everything in nature is part of one great network of living relationships.

Human beings, George Carver understood, are part of nature's network, too. As a professor of agriculture at the Tuskegee Institute, Carver taught his students and the farmers of southern Alabama how to work with nature to make worn-out farmland productive again. Long before other people began to speak about the problems of the environment, George Washington Carver was a pioneer in ecology.

He was also a deeply religious man. Carver believed that nature was the work of a "Great Creator." The Creator "talks to us through the things that he has created," Carver wrote. To him, the natural world was more than an object of scientific interest. The living things of the world were, in his view, "little windows through which God permits me to commune with Him."

Carver's message was one of hope, a message for the future. "I am interested in young people," he once wrote. "They must catch the vision." He wanted his work to be continued by the young people he thought of as his family.

"I am not a finisher," Carver admitted. "I am a blazer of trails. Others must take up the various trails of truth, and carry them on."

Chapter 2

The Plant Doctor

The boy who would be known as George Washington Carver was born the son of a slave. No one is certain of his birth date, however, because careful records of slave births were not kept. Most likely, it was in the spring of 1865, near the end of the Civil War. Throughout his life, George Washington Carver would note that he was born "just as freedom was declared."

Carver knew very little about his family history. His father was probably a slave on a nearby farm, but George never met him. "I am told," Carver wrote many years later, "that my father was killed while hauling wood with an ox team. In some way, he fell from the load under the wagon, both wheels passing over him."

George's mother, Mary, was a slave on a farm owned by Moses and Susan Carver. The Carvers had moved to Diamond Grove, Missouri, about 1838. They were among the first people to settle the vast prairie of southwestern Missouri, so their land was among the best. The Carvers had plenty of water and timber, and they owned 240 acres of the region's most fertile farmland.

When the Carvers arrived in Diamond Grove, they lived in a small, one-room cabin. They worked the rich, brown prairie land and slowly transformed it into fields of wheat and oats, productive orchards and beehives, and thriving vegetable gardens. In their broad pastures, Moses Carver's long-legged racehorses nibbled shoots of green grass, and cows slept under the trees.

By 1855, the Carver farm had become so prosperous that Moses and Susan could no longer run it without someone else's help. But Carver could not find anyone to hire. So even though Moses Carver was opposed to slavery, he purchased George's mother, Mary, then just 13 years old, from a neighbor. Moses Carver bought Mary for the sum of $700.

For four years, Mary was the Carvers' only slave. In 1859, Mary gave birth to a son, whom she named Jim. About six years later, she gave birth to George.

By the time George was born, the Civil War was in its final stages. The population of Missouri was equally divided in support of the North and the South. As a result, the people of Missouri were attacked by raiding parties from both sides.

During one of these raids, Mary and the infant George were kidnapped by southern supporters from the nearby state of Arkansas. Moses Carver contacted a neighbor, a Union scout named John Bentley, and asked him to track down the kidnappers.

Bentley followed the trail of the kidnappers. Although he could not find Mary, he was able to locate and bring back George. Moses Carver rewarded Bentley with one of his best racehorses.

George was a sickly baby, and the kidnapping had not helped his condition. He later wrote, "I was so very frail and sick that they thought, of course, that I would die within a few days." The Carvers moved the orphaned George and Jim into their own cabin, and Susan Carver cared for the infant.

George Washington Carver remained small and weak for much of his childhood. He later remembered his early years as "a constant battle between life and death."

As a slave, George did not have a last name. Slaves were considered the property of their owners, and George was called Carver's George. When the slaves were freed at the end of the war, the boys took the last name of their former owners.

In many ways, the Carvers treated George and Jim like family. George would later write that "Mr. and Mrs. Carver were very kind to me."

Although his memories of growing up on the Carver farm were happy ones for the most part, George Carver always felt the sadness of being without his mother. As a young child, he was often found standing beside Mary's spinning wheel.

"There are some things," he later said, "that an orphan child does not want to remember."

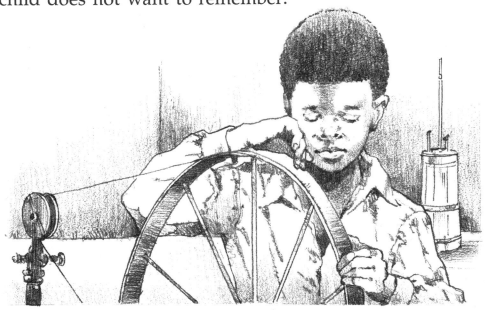

The Carvers were quiet, independent-minded people. They were well respected for managing such a profitable farm. Moses Carver was described as kind, though some people considered him a bit odd. He liked to play his violin for passersby, and he often gave the local children treats of honey from his beehives. Carver also entertained them by getting squirrels to eat out of his hand. He even had a pet rooster that sat on his shoulder.

As Jim and George grew, they took on chores around the Carver farm. Jim, who was athletic and strong, helped Moses with the heavy labor. Together, they would plant and harvest oats, potatoes, and other crops.

George was too frail for such work. He did most of his chores around the house and barnyard. George helped Susan with the cooking, cleaning, and laundry. He also learned how to do needlework and spent time planting and tending the vegetable garden.

When George was not performing his chores, he was free to explore the Carver farm. He spent many hours roaming through the nearby prairie and forests. He trotted alongside the wooded riverbanks, listening to the birds and watching the wild animals. Often, he would collect plants, rocks, and little creatures that caught his interest.

George took his treasures back home with him. One day, while Susan Carver was working in the house, she suddenly found herself surrounded by a cloud of feathery objects. One of George's milkweed pods had burst open and sent its light, silky seeds showering through the cabin. After that, the young collector had to leave his treasures at the door.

As George grew, so did his love of plants and flowers. He planted a secret flower garden at the edge of the woods not far from the cabin.

Every day, George would spend hours collecting new flowers and carefully tending his beloved plants. As he later wrote, "Many are the tears I shed because I would break the roots or flower off of some of my pets while removing them from the ground."

George did not want anyone to find out about his garden because, as he wrote, "it was considered foolishness in that neighborhood to waste time on flowers." But when the neighbors took notice of his skills, they began to bring their sick plants to George. He became known as the "plant doctor."

Along with his deep love of nature, George also began to develop an interest in religion. He recalled that when he was about eight years old, he learned about Sunday school and prayer from a playmate. When his friend went home, George tried to pray, and as he remembered, "God just came into my heart."

With God in his heart, George began to view the world around him in a new way. He saw nature as the work of the "Great Creator." Young George decided that in order to know God better, he would have to learn as much as he could about God's creation. "I wanted to know every strange stone, flower, insect, bird, or beast," he recalled. "I wanted to know where it got its color, where it got its life. But there was no one to tell me."

George first asked the Carvers to teach him what he wanted to know. Susan taught him to read from her old spelling book, and he studied it until he "almost knew the book by heart," as he later said. But that only made George want to learn more. "I sought the answers to my questions, but all in vain," he wrote.

Next, the Carvers tried to enroll George in the school in Diamond Grove. But he was turned away because the white townspeople would not permit a black child to go to school with their children. The Carvers hired a private tutor for a while, but he did not know much more than George did.

"My soul thirsted for an education," George recalled. The young boy realized that he would have to leave home if he wanted to get a real education.

In 1877, at about the age of 12, George left Diamond Grove. He headed to Neosho, Missouri, a town about eight miles away, where there was a school for black children. He left home with the Carvers' blessing and made the journey alone.

In Neosho, George was taken in by a black couple, Andrew and Mariah Watkins. In exchange for room and board, he helped with the chores when he was not in class. Mariah Watkins, a nurse and midwife, appreciated George's love of living things and taught him how to make simple medicines from plants.

A stern and demanding woman, Mrs. Watkins also taught young George that time was not to be wasted. He raced home during the school recess to study and to do laundry chores.

George Carver soon learned all he could in Neosho's one-room schoolhouse. At the end of a year, it was time for George to move on. He could not have known that his quest for an education had just begun.

Carver spent the next 10 years "drifting here and there as a ship without a rudder," as he later said. He continued to earn a living by doing odd jobs, always managing to find someone who needed a cook or some laundry work done. In his spare time, Carver played music, began painting, and kept up his custom of taking solitary walks to explore the countryside.

By 1885, Carver decided that he was ready to go to college. He applied to Highland College in Kansas and was accepted through the mail. However, when he arrived to begin classes, Carver was turned away. Highland did not admit black students. Once again, George Washington Carver went wandering in search of an education.

Finally, sometime between the years 1888 and 1890, Carver's travels brought him to the small town of Winterset, Iowa. He set up a laundry business and got to know the town and its inhabitants. It was during a church service that George Carver's singing caught the notice of a Mrs. Milholland. She and her husband immediately took an interest in the young man.

Carver was a frequent guest in the Milholland home. They delighted in George's creativity. As he later recalled, they "encouraged me to sing and paint, for which arts I had passionate fondness." In fact, the Milhollands were so impressed with Carver's talents that they persuaded him to try again for a college education.

In 1890, George Carver applied to Simpson College in Indianola, Iowa. On September 9, he finally began his college studies. He was the only black student on campus. Once again, he supported himself by doing laundry.

His fellow students were soon won over by Carver's warm personality and obvious talents. "They made me believe I was a real human being," Carver said of his classmates. He reported to the Milhollands that "the people here are very kind to me and the students are wonderfully good." Throughout his life, George Carver displayed an ability to make lasting friendships wherever he went.

At Simpson College, he made friends with some of the Indianola townspeople. He was especially close to the Listons, a white couple who owned the local bookstore. He spent many hours reading in the bay window of the Liston home.

Carver studied many different subjects at Simpson, but his best and favorite was art. His art teacher, Etta Budd, noted that "painting was in him." However, she hesitated to encourage Carver in the subject. She realized that it would be almost impossible for a black man to make a living as an artist.

Budd noticed that many of Carver's paintings had the same subject—plants. She admired the intricate detail of his drawings. Carver also brought her examples of plants that he had grown.

Budd encouraged Carver to change his course of study to botany, the study of plants. And she urged him to apply to Iowa State College of Agriculture and Mechanic Arts in Ames, Iowa, where her father was a professor of horticulture (the science of growing plants).

Carver decided that his teacher was probably right. As he wrote at the time, "I realize that God has a great work for me to do." Art, he now felt, would not be that great work.

George Carver wanted to do something that would benefit other African Americans. He had come to believe that nothing would help his people as much as a thorough knowledge of the science of agriculture.

George Washington Carver left Indianola in 1891. He was traveling again. But his years of restless searching were almost over.

Chapter 3

Nature's Agent

On the campus of Iowa State, Carver was once again the only black student. At first, he was the object of racial insults. In a letter to Mrs. Liston, Carver complained about the way he was being treated. "I put on my best hat and dress and took the train for Ames," an angry Mrs. Liston said. Carver reported that Mrs. Liston "walked out all over the campus" with him.

"The next day everything was different," Carver later wrote to Mrs. Liston. "The ice was broken, and from then on, things went very much easier."

Besides doing well in his class work—Carver was the school's outstanding botany student—he joined in many campus activities. He became a member of the German and art clubs and the debating society. He helped to start the campus agriculture society and student prayer meetings. And once the ice was broken, the "Doctor," as he was called, made friends easily.

Carver also continued to paint the plants that he found so fascinating. In 1892, some of his friends convinced Carver to enter his "Yucca and Cactus" painting in a statewide art contest in Cedar Rapids, Iowa. Then, after buying him a new suit, they took Carver to the train station and handed him a ticket to Cedar Rapids. His painting won first prize and was chosen to represent Iowa in a nation-wide fair in Chicago the next year.

Iowa State was the perfect place for Carver to study agriculture. By the time he arrived there, the school was a leader in agriculture education and research. The faculty even included two future secretaries of agriculture, James Wilson and Henry C. Wallace. Carver had finally found a school where the teachers knew more about plants than he did.

The need to improve farming practices was apparent to most farmers. With each passing year, the land was less and less productive. Many fields were ruined by deep gullies. The spring and winter rains washed away fertile topsoil. And what the rain didn't wash into the rivers, the wind blew away.

When Europeans came to America in the early 1600s, the land was dark and rich. For thousands of years, the soil had been almost untouched. When plants and animals died, they decomposed, or rotted, enriching the soil with their nutrients. The Indians had taken care of the land, only farming small plots of it at a time. And they would fertilize the soil—by planting a dead fish beside the corn seed, for instance. After a few years, their fields became woods or prairie land again.

The early settlers thought that there would always be more land than could be used. They chopped down the forests and burnt the grasses on the prairie land. They farmed a plot of land for only a few years. When a field was no longer productive, they moved on to a new one. They did not think about fertilizing the land (putting the nutrients that plants need back into the soil). They did not care about erosion (the wearing away of the soil by the action of wind and water).

Some farmers saw that the soil could not survive this treatment. In the early 1700s, Jared Eliot, a Connecticut minister and farmer, suggested that farmers plant crops that put nutrients back in the soil. Eliot also recommended that farmers rotate their crops, or plant different crops in a field from year to year. Samuel Deane, the author of *The New England Farmer*, which was published in 1790, thought that farmers should fertilize their fields with the manure from their cattle.

But most farmers thought taking care of the land was not very important. President Thomas Jefferson noted that part of the problem was that "we can buy an acre of new land cheaper than we can manure an old one." For almost

300 years, Americans had been careless with the land. In 1797, President George Washington reported to Congress that, with the increasing population, farming was becoming a matter of public concern.

Washington suggested that there should be a government agency to promote agriculture research. In this way, scientific knowledge about agriculture could be given to farmers, Washington said, "in a spirit of discovery and improvement."

By the mid-1800s, farmers were looking to the government to help them save the soil. In response, the U.S. Department of Agriculture was established in 1862. In that same year, the federal Land-Grant College Act was passed. Through this act, the federal government gave land to the states so that they could establish colleges "for the benefit of agriculture."

Twenty-five years later, in 1887, the Hatch Act gave money for these colleges to add experimental farms. On these agricultural experiment stations, scientists could test new ideas for farming, for fighting plant and animal diseases, and for raising poultry and livestock.

At Iowa State, George Washington Carver was known for his work with plants. His "green thumb" won him the respect of both students and professors.

Carver enjoyed his work. He also enjoyed early morning walks through the Iowa countryside. Alone, he would draw the prairie scene or sketch the morning freshness of a summer flower. He brought along an old metal can for specimens—insects and plants he wanted to study. During these quiet rambles, Carver waited for the natural world to reveal its secrets to him.

The secrets that he discovered convinced Carver that everything in the natural world is part of a "great whole." Every animal, every plant has an important role to play in nature's network of living things. It is as if the natural world were a vast jigsaw puzzle. Each living thing, Carver believed, is a piece of this great puzzle. No other piece, he wrote, "will fit exactly as well."

As a part of nature's network, human beings must work with nature in an environmental partnership, Carver insisted. The condition of America's farmland in Carver's time is a good example of what can happen when people forget that important lesson.

The fact that people depend on nature did not mean to Carver that they should be afraid to improve it. He wrote that "man is simply nature's agent or employee to assist her in her work." Carver was especially interested in ways to make nature more productive. In 1893, Carver published an article on the cactus. The tough, prickly cactus plant might seem to be of little use. But to George Carver, there was nothing in nature that was useless.

Nature does not make waste material, he wrote. Each living thing has a wide range of usefulness. Sometimes, he said, the uses of living things are "locked up within them," as if they are "waiting for the kindly hand of man to wave his magic wand over them that they may show forth their long hidden usefulness."

At the Iowa State experimental farm station, George Washington Carver served as nature's agent. He studied the unseen processes of nature so that he could bring out the "long hidden usefulness" of living things. His experiments involved two techniques: grafting, a process that joins two plants together, and cross-breeding, a procedure by which a new plant (called a hybrid) is produced by breeding, or mating, two different kinds of plants.

George Carver finished his undergraduate studies in 1894. His professors were so impressed with his research that they urged him to stay on and get his master's degree. Carver was appointed to the faculty as a teaching assistant and given the job of running the school greenhouse.

Carver's students must have been surprised by the man who stood before them. For most of them, this was the first time they had seen a black teacher. And George Carver was no ordinary teacher. His high-pitched voice and wrinkled suit (always with a fresh flower in the lapel) set him apart from the other professors.

But George Washington Carver was a gifted teacher, one who easily earned the respect and admiration of his students. Carver encouraged them to discover things for themselves. He expected his students to learn the way he had—through first-hand observation.

Not all of Carver's teaching was done in the classroom. He took his students on nature rambles. One "student" was a bit young for college. Six-year-old Henry A. Wallace, the son of Professor Henry C. Wallace, was also allowed to go on nature walks with Carver.

Years later, Henry A. Wallace recalled "many a Saturday afternoon collecting plant specimens in the woods and fields" at Carver's side. Carver's young student grew

up to be a botanist himself and a professor at Iowa State. He later became secretary of agriculture and vice president under Franklin D. Roosevelt. But Wallace never forgot the man he described as "the kindliest, most patient teacher I ever knew." He wrote that Carver "could cause a little boy to see the things which he saw in a grass flower."

Carver's own observations about the natural world were an important part of his graduate studies. He had been assigned to work with a professor of mycology, the study of fungi (primitive plants such as mushrooms) and the plant diseases that they cause. Little was known about fungi, so much of Carver's research involved gathering specimens to study.

As in other areas of botany, Carver displayed a great talent for mycology. He wrote two articles on the subject and collected more than 1,500 different specimens. His professor called him "the best collector I ever had in the department or have ever known."

Through his research, George Carver became known to agriculture departments throughout the country. As he was completing his Master of Agriculture degree, Carver began to receive job offers from other institutions.

The professors at Iowa State made it clear that they wanted Carver to stay right where he was. Professor James

Wilson, head of the agriculture department, spoke for the faculty when he said, "I would never part with a student with so much regret as George Carver. It will be difficult, in fact impossible, to fill his place."

Although Carver was happy at Iowa State, he looked forward to helping other African Americans improve their living conditions. He was especially interested in the offer that he received from Booker T. Washington, the founder of the Tuskegee Institute. Washington thought that the best way for black Americans to overcome racial prejudice was to learn the practical skills that would enable them to become productive members of society.

Washington wanted the students of Tuskegee to learn what he described as "the common occupations of life." As blacks began to climb the ladder of economic success, Washington argued, racial equality would follow.

In April 1896, George Washington Carver accepted a position at Tuskegee. He wrote to Washington that he hoped to teach new and better agriculture methods to poor southern blacks. "To this end," Carver said, "I have been preparing myself for these many years, feeling as I do that this line of education is the key to unlock the golden door of freedom to our people."

Chapter 4

Scientific Agriculture

The road to Tuskegee, Alabama, was a long one, a thousand miles from the sweeping grasslands of Iowa. But for George Washington Carver, the route was long in other ways, too. For the first time, Carver would be living in the South; for the first time, he would be living around other black people.

In his new home, George Carver quickly came to see how southern blacks were held down by poverty and held back by racism.

By the time Carver arrived in Alabama, slavery had been outlawed for more than 30 years. For many blacks, however, freedom had made little change in their lives.

Though the U.S. Constitution guaranteed blacks equal rights, throughout the South they were treated as second-class citizens. Many states passed laws to keep the races apart. These "Jim Crow" laws, named after a character in a folk song, required separate public facilities—schools, restaurants, movie theaters, parks, and playgrounds—for whites and blacks.

In 1896, in a case called *Plessy v. Ferguson*, the U.S. Supreme Court upheld this policy, ruling that blacks could be forced to use separate facilities as long as these facilities were equal to those available to whites. In fact, however, the facilities provided to whites were always far superior to those for blacks.

The Constitution may have guaranteed equal rights, but the southern system of land ownership guaranteed a life of debt and poverty for African Americans. Few blacks owned the land they worked. Instead, they rented land from white owners, paying them a share of the crop.

But this sharecropping system left little for the black farmers themselves, forcing them to borrow money to pay their expenses. Each year, the black farmer went deeper and deeper into debt.

The situation for black farmers was made worse by their own farming techniques. In desperate need of money, they planted cotton—a crop they could sell easily—year after year. This practice robbed the soil of nutrients, leaving the land less and less productive and trapping the black farmer in a world of poverty. Much of the soil in the South, Carver declared, "was practically a pile of sand and clay."

In October 1896, George Washington Carver arrived at the Tuskegee Institute. From his seat on the train, he could easily see the signs of economic hardship. Before him, Carver saw "a vast territory of barren and furrowed hillsides and wasted valleys."

This was indeed, as Carver said, "a new world."

The campus of Tuskegee—the place Carver would call home for the rest of his life—rose out of the Alabama countryside. Carver had been hired to oversee agriculture research at the school's experimental farm.

But as soon as he arrived at Tuskegee, he found that his job was going to be more difficult. Besides heading the agriculture department, the experiment station, and the two school farms, Carver was responsible for teaching several classes, landscaping the campus, and even serving as the school veterinarian.

He soon made the first of many angry complaints to Booker T. Washington. "I have labored early and late and at times beyond my physical strength," Carver wrote.

The heavy workload was bad enough, but Carver was expected to do all of these things with only a few assistants and with very little funding. The experimental farms at

white schools, like the one at Iowa State, received 10 times the amount of money that was provided to the Tuskegee station. "Here I am working with the smallest staff of any station in the United States," Carver complained.

"It is impossible for me to do this work," he continued, "without men and means."

Nonetheless, without men or means, Carver went to work. His first stop was the school garbage dump. "I went to the trash pile at Tuskegee Institute," Carver said, "and started my laboratory with bottles, old fruit jars, and any other thing I found I could use." Letting nothing go to waste, he fashioned a makeshift laboratory—"God's Little Workshop," he called it.

On the 10 acres of land that he was given for his farm station, Carver set out to save the soil. This meant learning how to work with nature instead of against it.

Carver worked on three ways to rescue the southern farmer from a history of bad farming and a future of poverty: using organic fertilizers to enrich the soil, rotating crops to prevent the soil from becoming worn out, and planting crops that return nutrients to the soil.

Carver wanted farmers to make fertilizers from the organic, or natural, things they were used to throwing away. These resources were free and plentiful. "Too much stress cannot be laid upon this important item," he said. Carver asked his students to make a heap out of "weeds, grass, leaves, pine tag, wood ashes, old plaster, lime, old clothing, shoes, broken up bones, feathers, hair, horns and hoofs of animals, swamp muck." In the summer heat, the waste slowly decomposed, leaving nutrient-rich material called compost.

Another source of natural fertilizer were the stalks and vines of harvested plants. These could be plowed under to enrich the fields of southern farmers. This method of fertilization was called green manuring. Carver declared that these two methods of organic fertilization—composting and green manuring—were "the cheapest and most effective way of reclaiming barren land."

But Carver knew that no amount of fertilizer would be enough if the same crops, needing the same nutrients, were planted in the same fields year after year. He urged farmers to plant more than one crop and to change the place they planted a crop from one season to another. By rotating the selection and placement of crops, the farmer allows the soil to store up nutrients for the future.

Instead of cotton, Carver suggested, why not plant legumes, such as cowpeas, velvet beans, soybeans, and peanuts? These crops actually return nutrients to the soil. By planting them, Carver explained, the farmer is "feeding" the soil with the things it will need for the next year's crop—he is saving the soil for another year. The farmer is also harvesting a crop that he can feed his family and livestock with, making him less dependent on things he has to buy.

At the experiment station, Carver demonstrated how well soil building and crop rotation can work. In the spring of 1897, he selected an acre of the poorest land on the farm. He planted soil-building legumes, and he used the

organic fertilizer made at his students' compost heap. The first year, he lost $2.40.

Carver was not discouraged, however. It had taken years to wear out the soil. And he knew that it would take years to build it up again. In 1903, that same plot of ground earned $94.65.

By applying scientific research to agriculture, George Washington Carver enabled poor southern farmers to farm productively and to preserve the soil so that it could be used for generations to come.

Although Carver complained about limited funding at the experiment station, the shortage of funds may have turned out to be a benefit. Because he could not afford to try expensive farming techniques, Carver used methods that even the poorest farmer—the "man fartherest down," as Carver said—could afford. His experimental farm was known as the "little man's station."

But success on the campus of Tuskegee was not the same as success on the farms of the South. George Carver came to Tuskegee because, as he claimed, "it has always been the one great ideal of my life to be of the greatest good to the greatest number of my people possible."

Improving the life of "the common man" was part of Tuskegee's educational goal. To achieve that goal, Carver had to make his research known to southern farmers.

One way that Carver tried to do this was by producing a series of leaflets describing the progress that he was making in scientific agriculture. These "Bulletins," meant to help the farmer and his family, were distributed free. For more than 40 years, Carver published bulletins on

a great variety of subjects, such as "How to Build Up Worn Out Soils," "How to Make Cotton Growing Pay," "Increasing the Yield of Corn," and "The Pickling and Curing of Meat in Hot Weather."

Many farmers could not read and, therefore, could not take advantage of such bulletins. In the early days of the college, Booker T. Washington took weekend drives through the Alabama countryside to talk with farmers and answer their questions. But Washington could only reach a few people this way.

In 1892, Tuskegee Institute began an annual Farmers' Conference that brought the area's farmers together, as Booker T. Washington said, to "talk over their conditions and needs." When Carver joined the faculty at Tuskegee, he played an important role at these conferences.

Through his old professor, Secretary of Agriculture James Wilson, Carver was able to get free seeds from the government to pass out to the farmers. By getting farmers to plant their own vegetables, Carver encouraged them to get away from what he called "the store habit." He took farmers to the experiment station where they could witness for themselves what new agricultural techniques could produce.

"They openly expressed themselves as feeling more encouraged than they had ever felt before," Carver said. "They could see the actual work upon the ground."

In 1897, Carver began a series of monthly meetings, the Farmers' Institute, which brought together a group of farmers for more in-depth education. The success of these meetings convinced Carver to sponsor a yearly farmers' fair on the Tuskegee Institute campus. In 1904, Tuskegee began to offer a free "Short Course in Agriculture" during the winter, when most farmers could afford to leave the farm for a few days.

During these years, Carver continued Washington's weekend rides in the country, carrying samples of farm products and other materials to share with the farmers. In 1904, Washington suggested that a wagon be equipped as a "traveling agricultural school" to make regular trips to the Alabama countryside. Carver thought this "movable school" was an excellent idea. He devised a wagon that would unfold into displays of dairy equipment and farm operations. For those who could not come to Tuskegee, Tuskegee would go to them.

A New York banker, Morris K. Jesup, helped to fund the project, and thus it was called the "Jesup Agricultural Wagon." Thomas M. Campbell, one of Carver's students, began operating it on May 24, 1906. That summer, the Jesup Wagon stopped at the end of cotton patches and corn fields, at crossroads and country stores—any place where farmers could be brought together. (The Department of Agriculture was impressed by Campbell's work. With the encouragement of both Carver and Washington, the department appointed him as the government's first black demonstration agent.)

"To be of the greatest good to the greatest number of my people"—that was Carver's goal. At times, it seemed like an impossible goal, and Carver knew many moments of frustration and disappointment over the years.

But George Carver succeeded in bringing a message of ecology—and hope—to the people who most needed help. Secretary of Agriculture James Wilson followed his research and concluded that Carver had achieved his goal. "You are probably doing more good to southern people than any man in the South," Wilson wrote.

*"Keep your thoughts free from hate,
and you need have no fear."*

Chapter 5

Understanding Relationships

George Washington Carver found himself in a new world when he entered his first classroom at Tuskegee. His students were not the sort that Carver was used to at Iowa State.

The children of poor black farmers, they had come to Tuskegee to learn a trade that would earn them a decent living. They had seen their fathers and mothers sweat in the fields for little reward—they weren't much interested in Carver's agriculture lessons.

As at Iowa State, it did not take long for Carver's enthusiasm and obvious love of nature to win over his new students. Believing that every living thing is part of one "great whole," Carver always started with something that his students knew well and then moved on to something that they didn't know—what he called the "nearest related unknown." His students learned how the living

things in nature's network are related. Education was a process of "understanding relationships," Carver said.

Carver developed some unusual teaching methods to support this idea. Instead of having separate classes for chemistry, biology, or geography, Carver would pick a single object, such as the cowpea, for his students to study. The students might investigate how periods of rain and drought affected the plant's growth. At the same time, they learned about weather patterns. Then, they studied what rain water added to the soil and, eventually, to the cowpea. And so they learned about chemical reactions.

In this way, George Carver taught his students more than scientific facts. He gave them a view of nature that stressed the lesson of ecology—that living things depend on one another in a natural network of relationships.

To make this lesson clear, George Carver insisted on the need for his students to find things out on their own. Carver believed that learning should be an adventure, a source of discovery.

"He would never tell you a thing, never answer your questions," one of his students remembered. "He would ask you another question and lead you into the answer."

Another student praised Carver this way: "He taught me how to use my brain."

Carver encouraged his students to make their own observations of nature. He held competitions between his classes to see who could gather the most specimens.

Perhaps Carver himself described his idea of education best when he said, "Every teacher should realize that a very large proportion of every true student's work must be outside the classroom." For Carver, the whole world was a classroom.

He continued to take his own morning rambles in the woods. "When you would ask him why," one student remembered, "he would say, 'to talk with God and the flowers.' " Carver would always emerge from the woods with a fresh flower in his lapel, ready to share what he had seen or heard with his "children," as he often called his students.

George Washington Carver was a demanding teacher, but he also thought that learning should be fun. His good sense of humor made the classroom an enjoyable place. Once, a group of students tried to fool him by constructing a fake insect from parts of other insects. They brought their "specimen" to him and asked him to identify the strange new creature they had found. Carver was amused by his students' creation, but he identified the "specimen" correctly. It was a "humbug," he said.

Concerned with his students' lives, Carver's door was always open to his "children." Many of Carver's students stayed in contact with him long after they left Tuskegee. In their letters, they called him "Father," "Dad Carver," and "Daddy." Sometimes, they asked for advice or help in finding a job. Often, they wrote just to share the news of their lives. Carver always wrote back letters of support and encouragement.

Carver was greatly concerned about how his students would respond to the world outside Tuskegee. He knew the racism that they would face, and he feared that their hearts would become filled with hate. "Hate within will eventually destroy the hater," he told his students. "Keep your thoughts free from hate, and you need have no fear from those that hate you."

"When our thoughts—which bring actions—are filled with hate against anyone, we are in a living hell," Carver explained. "Holding good thoughts brings us happiness, success, and peace."

"Without genuine love of humanity, it is impossible to accomplish much."

Chapter 6

The Wizard of Tuskegee

George Washington Carver made his most important contribution to agriculture through his research and teaching, but he is most famous for the work that he conducted in his laboratory. His laboratory activities served the same purpose as his other work—helping "the man fartherest down," as he often said.

"Creative chemistry" is what George Carver called the process by which he made hundreds of products from simple plants. He discovered how to make more than 280 different products from the peanut, including breakfast cereal, milk, dye, flour, ice cream flavoring, rubber, soap, candy, paint, medicine, glue, gasoline, and instant coffee, among other things. He found that more than 150 products can be made from the sweet potato.

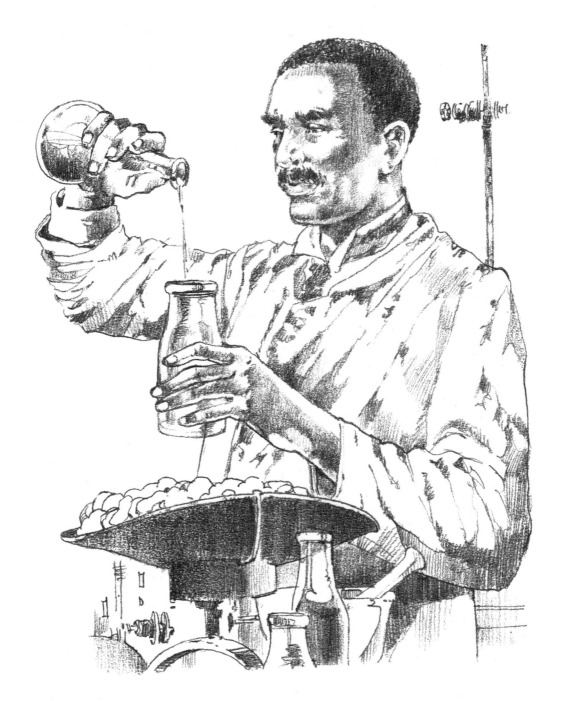

Carver's chemistry did not bring new industries to the South, as he had hoped, but it did help to make him famous. Countless stories were published about the man known as "The Wizard of Tuskegee" and "The Peanut Man." Other famous inventors, including Thomas Edison and Henry Ford, took an interest in Carver's work.

This publicity brought Carver invitations to speak at universities, social meetings, and county fairs across the South. Carver was a very entertaining speaker, and people flocked to hear him. "His name attached to a placard or bulletin announcing a farmers conference," said one conference official, "will draw a larger number of interested individuals—both white and black—than the name of any other speaker."

At such events, Carver always found a way to capture the attention of his audience. Wearing an old suit that had, as one friend noted, "that slept-in look," he tried to give his listeners the same sense of wonder about nature that he had known since childhood.

His sense of humor was a part of these events, too. Carver often told his audiences how he was inspired to begin his work with the peanut. According to Carver, he had asked "Mr. Creator" to reveal to him the secrets of the universe. But God had answered, "You want to know too much for that little mind of yours." So Carver asked to know the secrets of the earth, but God's answer was the same. Then, Carver asked to know the secrets of the humble peanut. The peanut, God said, was just the right size for George Washington Carver.

Not surprisingly, the leaders of the peanut industry thought that "The Peanut Man" would be a perfect spokesman for their product. They asked him to give a speech at a meeting of the United Peanut Association of America. There he "won his way into the hearts of the peanut men," according to the editor of the society's journal.

For several years, the Peanut Association had been asking Congress to put a tariff, or import tax, on foreign peanuts. Such a tax would protect the American peanut industry from foreign growers. The peanut men wanted Carver to plead their case to Congress.

On January 21, 1921, George Carver found himself in Washington, D.C., in front of the House Ways and Means Committee. The chairman of the committee said to him,

"All right, Mr. Carver, we'll give you 10 minutes." Carver proceeded to unload from his old, battered carrying case some of the many products he had made from peanuts. But he had barely started his presentation when he looked at his watch. His 10 minutes were up.

By that time, the congressmen were fascinated by the sight of so many products. One of them spoke up, saying, "This is interesting. I think his time should be extended." Indeed, it was extended several times until the chairman finally declared, "Your time is unlimited."

For the next hour, Carver talked about the variety of products set out before him. And not long after Carver spoke to the committee, Congress approved the tariff for the peanut industry.

George Carver's appearance in Washington drew the nation's—and the world's—attention. He became known as a brilliant and inventive scientist.

In 1916, Carver was asked to join the advisory board of the National Agricultural Society. In that same year, he became the only African-American member of Great Britain's prestigious scientific society, the Royal Society for the Arts. In 1918, he was appointed as a consultant to the U.S. Department of Agriculture.

Carver was honored by both white and black groups. The National Association for the Advancement of Colored People (NAACP) awarded him the Spingarn Medal for Distinguished Service to Science for his achievements in agriculture. By the 1920s, when Carver was in his fifties, there were few Americans who had not heard of "The Wizard of Tuskegee."

In the late 1920s, Carver began to work closely with the Commission for Interracial Cooperation (CIC) and the Young Men's Christian Association (YMCA). These student groups asked Carver to give a series of lectures to mostly white audiences. They hoped that Carver's warm personality and fascinating work would help to promote good race relations in the South.

Apparently, Carver was successful on these speaking tours. He brought a number of white students into his family of followers—and he changed their lives. One of Carver's white "children" wrote to him, "You have shown me the one race—the human race."

Carver himself was often the victim of racist attitudes. When he addressed the Peanut Association in 1920, for instance, Carver had to ride the freight elevator to the meeting room. The passenger elevator was reserved for whites only.

But Carver never let racial prejudice make him angry or bitter. "Without genuine love of humanity," he insisted, "it is impossible to accomplish much in this question of the races."

On January 5, 1943, George Washington Carver died. He was almost 80 years old.

George Carver was buried near Booker T. Washington on the grounds of the Tuskegee Institute. The epitaph on his headstone is a fitting summary of the man and his life's work:

"He could have added fortune to fame, but caring for neither, he found happiness and honor in being helpful to the world."

Chapter 7

The Secret of True Happiness

George Washington Carver came to Alabama to help the poor farmers of the South. The value of his teaching and research, however, stretched far beyond the borders of southern Alabama. They continue today through such institutions as the George Washington Carver Museum at the Tuskegee Institute.

The American public is reminded of his importance at the George Washington Carver National Monument in Diamond Grove, Missouri, which marks his birthplace and childhood home. Carver's picture is on a postage stamp, and many schools, public buildings, and even a nuclear submarine bear his name.

Carver was elected to the Agricultural Hall of Fame. He was the second African American enshrined in the Hall of Fame for Great Americans. (The first was Tuskegee founder Booker T. Washington.)

64

The message that George Washington Carver tried to convey, in the classroom and in the countryside, was a message of ecology—the idea that everything in nature is part of one great whole. Whether he was talking about a vegetable garden or the human family, Carver believed that we are part of a network of relationships.

If people could only learn to understand and cooperate with these relationships, if they could learn to work with nature, then, Carver thought, they would be happy.

"To those who have as yet not learned the secret of true happiness," he wrote, "begin now to study the little things in your own door yard."

George Washington Carver was an environmentalist before that word was ever used. The earth, in his words, is "not just a treasure house to be ransacked and plundered and to be profited from." It is, he said, "our home and a place of beauty and mystery and God's handiwork."

Products
Created by George Washington Carver
from Peanuts

BEVERAGES

Blackberry punch

Cherry punch

Evaporated peanut beverage

Peanut punch

COSMETICS

Antiseptic soap

Face cream

Glycerine

Hand lotion

Oil for hair and scalp

Shampoo

Shaving cream

DYES, PAINTS, AND STAINS

Dyes for leather and cloth

Paints

Wood stains

FOODS FOR FARM ANIMALS

Hen food

Molasses feed

Peanut hay meal

Peanut hull bran

Peanut hull meal

Peanut meal

Peanut stock food

FOODS

Bar candy

Bisque powder

Breakfast food

Butter (from peanut milk)

Buttermilk

Caramel

Cheese cream

Chili sauce

Chocolate-coated peanuts

Chop suey sauce

Cocoa

Cooking oil

Cream candy

Cream from milk

Crystallized peanuts

Curds

Instant coffee

Mayonnaise

Mock chicken

Mock meat

Pancake flour

Peanut brittle

Peanut butter

Peanut cakes

Peanut chocolate fudge

Peanut flour

Peanut meal

Peanut milk

Peanut relish

Peanut tofu sauce

Peanut wafers

Salad oil

Vinegar

Worcestershire sauce

MEDICINES

Emulsion for bronchitis

Iron tonic

Laxatives

Medicine similar to castor oil

Quinine

GENERAL

Axle grease

Charcoal from peanut shells

Cleaner for hands

Fuel briquettes

Gasoline

Glue

Illuminating oil

Insecticide

Insulating boards

Linoleum

Lubricating oil

Nitroglycerine

Paper

Plastics

Printer's ink

Rubber

Soil conditioner

Products
Created by George Washington Carver
from Sweet Potatoes

FOODS

After dinner mints

Bisque powder

Breakfast food

Candies

Chocolate

Flour

Granulated potatoes

Instant coffee

Lemon drops

Meal

Mock coconut

Molasses

Orange drops

Sauce

Spiced vinegar

Starch

Sugar

Synthetic ginger

Tapioca

Vinegar

Yeast

FOODS FOR FARM ANIMALS

Hog feed

Stock feed meal

GENERAL

Alcohol

Fillers for wood

Library paste

Medicine

Paints and dyes

Paper (from vines)

Rubber compound

Shoe blacking

Synthetic cotton and silk

Writing ink

Some Key Bulletins Produced by George Washington Carver

1898	Feeding Acorns
1898	Experiments with Sweet Potatoes
1899	Fertilizer Experiment with Cotton
1903	Cow Peas
1905	Cotton Growing on Sandy Upland Soils
1905	How to Build Up Worn-Out Soils
1906	Successful Yields of Small Grain
1906	Saving the Sweet Potato Crop
1907	Saving the Wild Plum Crop
1908	Relations of Weather and Soil Conditions to the Fruit Industry of Southeast Alabama
1908	How to Cook Cow Peas
1909	Increasing the Yield of Corn
1909	Some Ornamental Plants of Macon Co., Alabama
1910	Possibilities of the Sweet Potato in Macon County
1910	Nature Study and Gardening for Rural Schools
1912	The Canning and Preserving of Fruits and Vegetables in the Home
1912	Dairying in Connection with Farming
1916	How to Grow the Peanut and 105 Ways of Preparing It for Human Consumption
1917	Twelve Ways to Meet the New Economic Conditions Here in the South
1918	How to Grow the Tomato and 105 Ways to Prepare It for the Table
1927	How to Make and Save Money on the Farm
1935	The Raising of Hogs
1936	How to Build Up and Maintain the Virgin Fertility of Our Soils
1938	Some Choice Wild Vegetables that Make Fine Foods
1942	Nature's Garden for Victory and Peace

Glossary

agriculture the science of producing crops and raising animals; farming

botany the scientific study of plants

compost a mixture of decaying matter, such as leaves or manure, that is used as fertilizer

conservation the process by which natural resources are saved, or conserved

cross-breeding the procedure by which a plant (called a hybrid) is produced by mating different kinds of plants

decompose to decay or rot

ecology the study of living things in their environment

environment the physical world that surrounds a plant or animal

environmentalist a person who seeks to protect the natural environment

erosion the wearing away of rock or soil by the action of water and wind

farming the cultivation of the land for the production of crops

fertilizer material that is added to the soil to make plants grow better

grafting	a process that joins together parts of two plants
green manuring	plowing under the stems and vines of plants in order to fertilize the soil
horticulture	the science of growing plants
hybrid	a plant that is produced by the breeding, or mating, of two different kinds of plants
mycology	the study of fungi (primitive plants such as mushrooms) and the diseases they cause
organic	a substance derived from living things; natural
preservation	the process by which an environment is kept, or preserved, in its natural condition
restoration	the process by which a damaged environment is restored to its natural condition
rotation	the process by which a farmer changes the placement of a crop from year to year
sharecropping	when a farmer pays a share of his or her crop as rent
specimen	a sample insect or plant for study
topsoil	the part of the earth's surface in which plants grow
waste	material that is useless or worthless, such as garbage or trash
wildlife	animals or plants living in a natural state

Index